Compensation Systems, Job Performance, and How to Ask for a Pay Raise

Compensation Systems, Job Performance, and How to Ask for a Pay Raise

Dr. Paulett Hemmings Ph.D.

To order additional copies of this book, contact:
Xlibris
1-888-795-4274
www.Xlibris.com
Orders@Xlibris.com
735065

Compensation Systems, Job Performance,

And How to Ask for a Pay Raise

Dr. Paulett Hemmings Ph.D.

ABOUT THE AUTHOR

PAULETT HEMMINGS IS the CEO of 360 Performance Solutions (360performancesolutions.com) consulting company, and she teaches business professionals how to be outstanding leaders. Her area of expertise is organizational improvement and human resource management. As an undergraduate, Paulett attended Pace University in New York, where she received her BBA in General Management. She furthered her studies and graduated from Long Island University, New York with an MBA in Management. Paulett earned her Ph.D. in Organization and Management from Capella University and recently graduated with a Post-Doctorate Certificate in Human Resource Management from Walden University, Minneapolis. Some of Paulett Hemmings' professional affiliations are the Society for Human Resource Management (SHRM), American Society for Quality (ASQ), National Association of Professional Women (NAPW), and American Association of University Professors (AAUP). Paulett is a NAPW VIP member and received the 2015-2016 Professional Woman of the Year Award for outstanding leadership and commitment within her profession.

FOREWORD

PROPER COMPENSATION AND reward systems are critical means to increase productive advantages for most organizations. Therefore, there is a need for various methodologies to be used in developing an organization's compensation benefits program. The purpose of this book is to analyze compensation and rewards, and to provide a guide on how to ask for a pay increase. Having a wide perspective on compensation, one is able to understand the different aspects that go into strategic business thinking and how the compensation package is organized.

It is important to note that employees may not be willing to dedicate time and effort to their work if they are not recognized for it, whether they are located locally or globally. They will, in turn, decrease productivity to compensate for their lack of appropriate pay and benefits. Solid reward packages need full consideration and attention in their development. Organizations should, therefore, deliberately create a reward package that supports retention, employee development, and quality of life in order to maintain strong performance and full productivity (Gross & Friedman, 2004). The productivity of the organization is connected to the total-rewards and also to the overall business strategy prepared and executed on an ongoing basis. Strategies should therefore be created to enable qualified employees to receive their reward at the appropriate time for the right reason.

PREFACE

EMPLOYEES PERFORM ASSIGNED tasks, and the organization pays them for their work productivity. Compensation involves an exchange of labor for pay and benefits, and both the employer and the employee gain value from this transaction. Compensation is comprised of many different types of rewards and recognitions. Reward systems include base pay, incentive, merit, vacation, sick pay, health insurance, and such things as cell phone, housing, or car allowance. Recognizing employee work contribution and acknowledging their accomplishments through service excellence, service awards, and others valuable appreciation help to motivate the workforce. The organization supports an employee's productivity through motivation, stimulation, self-improvement, and a commitment from the employer.

Compensations and rewards are sizeable expenses for any organization. Therefore, they must be handled carefully. Some organizations are unable to attract the right talent because their compensation and benefits programs are not reasonable. Today, organizations are focusing on core competencies and pay for performance for their employees. Therefore, employees should know that developing their skills, being team players, solving problems, and exemplifying leadership are some of the core competencies that organizations look for in making hiring and promotions decisions.

Every employee should understand the organization's mission and goals, and how their employment is connected to these. Employees should also know that their job responsibilities are linked to the need of the organization and that employees should possess the right skills, knowledge, and abilities to help achieve organizational objectives. Employers should reward and compensate their employees appropriately for their work efforts. In this regard, employers should understand that the pay workers receive is connected to their productivity, motivation, inspiration, and turnover. This book provides a clear understanding of the various rewards system many organizations may offer. It also outlines the connection between compensation, benefits, and employee motivation. Finally, it teaches employees how to ask for a pay increase.

DR. PAULETT HEMMINGS PH.D.

HOW TO USE THIS BOOK

T HE FIRST PART of this book focuses on compensation while the second part guides employees how to negotiate salary and pay increases. Both sections are to be used by every employee, as employees are business executives, managers, and line/staff workers. After reading the compensation section, an employee will know how management feels and plans for compensation. The knowledge gained will better guide them through the process of pay negotiation.

This book is not designed to give in-depth compensation and pay analysis. Rather, it serves to guide workers from one level to another starting from compensation to pay increase. Lower-level workers will, at some point, become leaders through development or formal education. This book can be used for many years to solve some compensation and pay issues.

The author used source citations as evidence to support the main topic of most paragraphs. For the most part, the author starts with a main idea, continue with supporting source evidence, then an explanation or analysis relating this evidence to the main idea, and conclude with a lead out summation of the paragraph.

For example, in chapter 1, the main idea is: employees accept a job offer by agreeing to a contract exchanging work in return for wages and benefits. The author provided the following as source evidence: Gagne and Forest (2008) discussed that, in the working relationship, the employer connects the employee's interest with the interest of the company and pays the employee for accomplishing an agreed-upon goal. Similarly, Hoffman (2014) stated that the state "has responsibilities as an employer to treat workers fairly, pay them fair wages, and pay the right people appropriate salaries" (p. 1). For analysis, the author noted that the more the relationship between the employer and employee flourishes, the stronger the interest of the employer is connected to the interest of the employee. A good relationship enables both parties to reap positive benefits. When there is a breakdown in relationship between either party, the contract is negatively affected, and the relationship becomes dysfunctional. Additionally paying employees their right salaries is of high interest. For the lead out summation, the author explained that the relationship between employer and the employee should be strong for longevity, productivity, and job satisfaction. The literature review is evaluation of prior research that compares and contrasts the findings or analysis. The author hopes you will gain a lot from reading this book.

DR. PAULETT HEMMINGS PH.D.

PART 1

CHAPTER 1

A) Employees Should be Compensated

EVERY ORGANIZATION IS developed through the work strategies, habits of the leaders, and the work efforts of the employees. The employees are the backbone of the organization. As employees are developed and become skillful in their field, each organization will reflect the development and skill of its workforce. For small businesses, the business owners are the backbone of the business; for partnerships, the partners are the backbone of the company; and for large organizations, executive leaders are the strategic visionaries, while employees perform the essential functions of the entity. A line person performs the core work responsibilities of the firm such as sales or production, while a staff person plays a supporting role such as human resource officer, or office manager. Every employee, regardless of their role, must be paid for their work accomplished.

Employees accept a job offer by agreeing to a contract exchanging for work in return for wages and benefits. Gagne and Forest (2008) discussed that, in the working relationship, the employer connects the employee's interest with the interest of the company and then pays the employee for accomplishing the agreed-upon goal. Similarly, Hoffman (2014) stated that the state "has responsibilities as an employer to treat workers fairly, pay them fair wages, and pay the right people appropriate salaries" (p. 1). The more the relationship between the employer and employee flourishes, the stronger the interest of the employer is connected to the interest of the employee.

Good relationship enables both parties to reap positive benefits. When there is a breakdown in relationship between either party, the contract is negatively affected, and the relationship becomes dysfunctional. The relationship between employer and the employee should be strong for longevity, productivity, and job satisfaction. Included in the work agreement is an understanding of improvement and productivity tied to a salary.

Employers want continuous peak performance from the employee to gain productive advantages. To enable productivity, the company should match the employee's performance with an appropriate salary. Hameed, Ramzan, Ali, and Arslan (2014) identified that a company's pay and reward systems can affect an employee's productivity in many ways. If the pay is not equitable, the employee may reduce productivity or consider working elsewhere. Alternatively, the company can improve the work environment or encourage the employee to work in an area of greater value and interest to the employee.

B) Statement of the Problem

Many organizations have performance difficulties stemming from lack of adequate pay, benefits, and creativity that employees are seeking. Employees, in turn, move from one organization to another in search of creativity and incentives that match their education and status. According to Gagne and Forest (2008), compensation systems affect the human psyche and are connected to job enjoyment, performance, and motivation. Accordingly, many employees believe that their compensation should be quantified based on their qualifications, job efforts, and experience. When employees do not view their compensation as fair, they become dissatisfied. In turn, they put less quality, time, and effort into their work and the organization is negatively affected.

C) Literature Review of Employee Compensation

To encourage work productivity and work engagement, some employers offer total rewards, which is a mixture of compensation, rewards, and work experience. Gagne and Forest (2008) articulated that employees receive compensation as payment for their work accomplished, and the reward is a mixture of fringe benefits (e.g. health insurance, a company car) and monetary value. Similarly, Applebaum and McKenzie (1996) stated that compensation is used to reward, preserve, and influence employees; while Gross, Bundy, and Johnson (2011) argued that some companies attract, retain, and motivate their employees with total-rewards that include work-life balance, and career development. Total-rewards are not always maintained to meet the employee's requirements, and the diminishing value of total-reward packages may cause some workers to move to other organizations. Therefore, organizations are to have a vision plan to use motivation, development, knowledge, creativity, and skills appropriately to stimulate job interest.

Some new employees negotiate the compensation and benefits package they think is equitable for their specific job requirements before they accept a new position. Additionally, other employees may accept the compensation package their employers offer without any negotiation. Some may not know the value of negotiation, while others may feel intimidated and unequipped to negotiate a comfortable rewards package.

Most employees cannot live on the same salary from year to year without an increase. For many decades, the cost of living has risen annually, and adjustments in salary on an annual basis help employees offset the higher cost of living. Ramamoorti and Balakrishnan (2010) discussed that a strategy for most organizations to maintain a good relationship with its employees is to provide a compensation program that steadily grows and also matches the organization's profile. Similarly, Hameed et al. (2014) argued that compensation should be devised so the pay is aligned with the educations and the pay system should be applied with ethics and compassion. In light of this, employers should show concern about their employee's welfare and treat them with sensitivity. Typically, organizations that demonstrate to their employees that they care about their well-being and meet their needs are sustainable businesses.

To provide the right compensation packages for employees, organizations must have a plan in place that allocates the needed funding on an annual basis. Lawler, (1995) explained that organizations use business strategies to guide the goals of the firm, and it is through business strategies that plans for employee rewards are funded. A business strategy is a long-term goal with steps of how to meet customer needs, how to generate revenues, and to sustain productive advantages in the market. Business strategies also take into consideration how to align the strategies and steps with the mission and vision of the organization.

The company mission says the purpose of the organization, the things the organization will do, and the steps to take to get them accomplished. The vision says where the company is heading for the present and future and the core values such as, what the firm believes in, its expectations, and the culture of the firm. Appelbaum and Mackenzie (1996) explained how mission and the vision of a business can be used to create compensation structure. Employee's compensation is part of the vision and principles of the organization, and salaries should be clearly outlined to encompass the responsibility, performance, competencies, development, and skill set of its employees. In light of these discussions, a certain percentage of the firm's profit earnings should be used to reward employees annually and should be set aside exclusively for that purpose.

In order to handle incremental changes that organizations go through, and for the organization to progress, the needs of the employees must also be met. Giving employees the pay they are worth allows them to put full effort toward their responsibilities to keep the company running smoothly. Gagne and Forest (2008) stated "when employees enjoy their job and are engaged, they reach optimal performance and optimal functioning" (p. 225). Engagement means that the worker is engaged with accomplishing the work tasks, is enthusiastic about work, and use creativity and tact in getting the work done on time. Optimal performance and function mean that the employee puts forth full effort, critical thinking, critical analysis, and his or her best to accomplish the objectives of the organization. On the other hand, Sita and Pinapati (2013) articulated that it is through competency that an employee's performance is improved. Employees who are satisfied with their salary and benefits take care of the assets of their organization more appropriately than those who are dissatisfied and disgruntled. It is, therefore, a necessary endeavor for the organization to encourage high expectations of the employees, to inspire motivation, and stimulate them to take on work innovations that will increase their self-esteem.

Every organization has a different plan for structuring compensation. Lawler (1995) argued that some employees choose an organization based on the type of reward it offers, and a higher volume of employees are attracted to companies that offer more rewards. Levy, Mitchell, Guled and Guled (2010), suggested that public sector employees in the United Kingdom (UK) receive better compensation, such as pay and pensions, than their counterparts in the private sector. Some firms thrive on employee retention, so they attract quality employees to enable their retention rate to increase. On the other hand, other firms may pay more rewards because the organizations are more demanding of employee's time, effort, and commitment. These organizations may need longer work hours, have work schedules that are outside of a nine-to-five schedule, or have a high volume of travel.

D) Summary

Without the employees, the organization cannot move forward, so it is imperative that the employee is developed and compensated appropriately. Employee compensation should be tied to business strategy, and salary allocation and increases should be part of the overall goal of the organization. To improve retention, salary increase is appropriate, and employee quality of life improvement is necessary.

CHAPTER 2

A) Competencies

ORGANIZATIONS WANT THEIR employees to achieve competency in their work activities, so their business can have performance and productive advantages. Competency is defined as having motives, beliefs, traits, skills, and attitudes that are connected to work-related activities (Chen & Naquin, 2006). A competent worker is a confident worker, and competence inspires the employee to desire new knowledge and new ways to process the work activities in an efficient manner. Work competencies improve the attitude of a person and translate to modified and improved behavior.

B) Performance-Based

Employers have a variety of pay formats to use in designing their incentive packages for their employees. Employers may choose base pay, while others offer performance-, skill-, or team-based pay structure.

Gagne and Forest (2008) reported that performance-based pay generates higher work outputs and more work enjoyment than employees who are paid with a base pay format. In contrast, Ramamoorti and Alakrishnan (2010) said that employees may engage in bad behaviors because they are motivated by the incentives and rewards offered.

To get acknowledgement and incentives, some employees may be inspired to be creative in showing proof that they have increased output, reduced cots, or made positive changes by using fradulent proof or information. Although some people may be inclined to misrepresent their performance, the reality is that performance-based pay encourages stronger performance, as the value of the work is based on employee accomplishments rather than their ability to show up for work on a daily basis. For the activities of the organization to be viewed as fair in the eyes of its employees, companies "also have to determine what type of performance will be rewarded, such as cost-reduction, volume productivity, mentoring of others, or sales increase" (Lawler, 1995, p. 17). When the employees are rewarded, and they know what the reward is generated from, they may be encouraged to continue that path or to develop higher competencies and work efforts to maintain quality performance. Identifying specific performance-based goals helps employees to see their paths, growth, competence, and accomplishments. Additionally, the goals also allow the employer to create a framework that can be modified periodically based on need.

C) Skill-Based

Another method of reimbursing employees for work is the skill-based approach. The level of employee skill used in accomplishing the work tasks is evaluated, and the efficiency of the work produced is taken into consideration. Murray and Gerhart (1998) articulated that some workers increase their skill level to earn higher salaries. Therefore, the employer should redesign these employees' work responsibilities so they can take on more work functions that need a higher degree of skills competence. In contrast, Lawler (1995) discussed that some organizations compensate some of their employees with above-the-market-pay-rate schemes to stimulate their interest and motivation. Top-tiered, good salaried employees are usually offset by the premium return on investment their work brings in. In these regards, employees apply their competency to their work functions to improve the performance of the organization and to meet its goals.

D) Team-Based

When compensation is team-based, employees support each other's work efforts and work productivity through their team effort. According to Gagne and Forest (2008), employees work together and share a bond in the completion of the work, rather than in individual accomplishments. The team uses different ideas and suggestions from its members to solve problems, create initiatives, and fulfill the requirements of the job. Similarly, Haines and Tagger (2006) said

DR. PAULETT HEMMINGS PH.D.

team-based pay motivates cooperation, integration, problem-solving, and development, while Lawler (1995) explained that in the team bonus plans, employees do not compete with each other. They instead support each other and share in the reward of the team as a whole. Therefore, teams require less supervision and are self-supporting in their work endeavors. Team-based pay reduces overall expense, as fewer supervisors are needed because the team governs itself for the most part.

Some employees are self-motivated and enjoy self-government. On the other hand, other employees enjoy working in teams where they can get the support of other members. Haines and Tagger (2006) discussed that team members expect shared rewards when they work with other team members to accomplish a job. Similarly, Appelbaum and Mackenzie (1996) said that the team is more efficient when there is collaboration and cohesiveness of all the members working together. Additionally, Gagne and Forest (2008) explained that when employees are paid based on group output, the satisfaction levels of the members increased. The result is team collectivism, where the team supports one another and work together to fulfill the objectives of the organization. The team members are rewarded based on the team effort. The reward demonstrates that when members of the organization collaborate and work together, great benefits can be reaped.

E) Bonus / Incentive Based

When employees work hard to achieve their job responsibilities and have worked over and above the call of duty, they like to be recognized and rewarded for their contributions. Applebaum and McKenzie (1996) stated that some employees are given cash incentive payments as an encouragement for continued job success and accomplishments. Some of these incentives are tied to increases in sales, increases in production, expense reductions, creativity, and innovative suggestions. Similarly, Kiyani, Akhtar, and Haroon (2011) explained that employees receive incentives for work performance that is commendable, and the reward could be in the form of bonuses, paid vacation time, stock options, and gain sharing. Workers are motivated to improve job processes and increase outputs when they know that their work is respected, recognized, and acknowledged. Incentives say to the employee, "I see your work, and I appreciate your efforts". These recognitions and rewards increase job enjoyment and help them feel valued.

F) Summary

Organizations have a variety of compensation systems that they may choose to use to compensate their employees. Some of these are base pay, team-, performance-, and skill-based pay. The employer decides which pay plan is best to use and then apply the pay system to meet the needs of the company.

CHAPTER 3

A) The Board of Directors

PUBLICLY TRADED COMPANIES have a responsibility to have strong fiscal and administrative oversight, so there are transparencies within the firm, and the shareholders are not misled. The board of directors is responsible for governing the organization, to lead the Chief Executive Officer (CEO), and to ensure compliances are facilitated in all day to day work activities. According to Berk and DeMazo, (2014) and Laux and Laux, (2009), the shareholders select a board of directors to: monitor the executives, approve major investments, hire the executive team, approve acquisitions, create executives' compensations, oversee financial reports, and protect the concerns of the shareholders. Having a board of directors encourages the stockholders to have more confidence in the organization and to expect development and productivity over the long term.

Organizations have complexities, and to assist the board with some of its duties, they hire a compensation committee and an audit committee with specific duties for them to oversee. Wood, (2004) and Laux and Laux (2009) said the compensation committee handles the executive compensation aspects, while, Laux and Laux (2009) said the audit committee monitors the honesty of the financial statements and the internal audit roles. Similarly, Ramamoorti and Alakrishnan (2010) explained that the compensation committee ensures that there are transparencies in the executive administrative processes, while the internal audit committee counsels the general counsel, human resource, risk officer, board members, and CEO ensure compliance. Laux and Laux (2009) noted that an important duty of the internal auditor is to prevent earnings management by the executives, who can sometimes focus on managing and increasing their stock portfolios instead of managing and increasing the organization's performance and profitability. Some companies may overstate their earnings and therefore, the financial report is necessary to verify the reliability of the information.

B) The Compensation Committee

All organizational executives receive compensations that are tailored differently than those of the lower-level employees. Some boards transfer the executive compensation packages and their performance targets to the guidance of a compensation committee (Schiehll, 2005; Wood, 2004; Laux & Laux, 2009). The committee is also responsible for reviewing executive performance, stock options, bonuses, and senior leaders' salary increases (Schiehll, 2005; Laux & Laux, 2009; & Wood, 2004). Furthermore, CEOs and the executive members receive rewards, for the most part, in stock options. The board of directors analyzes the job responsibilities and provides the right measure to assess the efficiency of the business executives. Laux & Laux (2009) argued that stock shares are given as an incentive to boost the performance of CEOs and the other executives. Similarly, Goh and Gupta (2010) stated that issuing stock-based compensation to reward executives is an effective manner of connecting their performance to their pay. In addition, Berk and DeMarzo (2014) explained that some executives' pay is based on the performance of the organization and the growth of the earnings through stock options. Sometimes, some CEOs and executives are motivated to increase the price of the stock shares to enhance their gains.

The CEOs and the executives are not able to use manipulative methods to increase the stock shares without the existence of loopholes within their organizations. If the board is doing its job to oversee the activities of the organization, the executives, and the value of the firm, then the executives will not have any method to engage in fraudulent activities. Therefore, a large responsibility rests on the shoulders of the board members to ensure that the organization is in compliance with all regulatory directives and that the CEO is making the right business decisions.

C) Executive Compensation

The CEO ensures that the firm is running smoothly, leaders are meeting strategic objectives, budgets are in order, fiscal plans are appropriate, and the organization is achieving productive advantages. The pay structure for the CEO is created and maintained by the board of directors (Schiehll, 2005; Berk & DeMarzo, 2014; Laux & Laux, 2009). The board ensures that all executives are working within the frame of all government compliances, and that the company's reputation is protected.

Executives are hired and promoted to perform responsibilities that will lead to improving the organization and building the reputation of the firm. The compensation committee sets the limit on the bonus each executive can earn at the end of the year, called the target bonus, and it is typically a proportion of the base pay (Schiehll, 2005). Executive compensation is a combination of shares, salary, and bonuses. Creating a bonus threshold demonstrates that the board is using compliance measures to prevent excessive payouts, and to identify ethical and unethical work practices. In addition, the bonuses are to be connected to the executive's work performance. Often times executives also get compensations that are non-cash, and that could include subsidized housing or mortgages, membership in health clubs or country clubs, and generous vacation time.

D) Summary

The board of directors oversees the organization, and they set standards for the CEO to follow while monitoring the progress of the organization. The compensation committee handles the CEO's and executives compensation and decides on the amount of stocks to offer them. Company executives including the CEO get a mixture of salary, stock shares, bonuses, and perks as part of their compensation package.

CHAPTER 4

A) Performance Measures

T HE CEO'S JOB is to lead the organization to reach high-performance through accomplishing goals and objectives. The organization department's goals and objectives are outlined in the annual strategic goals of the firm, and it is through these objectives and goals that the performance measures are decided. According to Schiehll, (2005) and Laux and Laux (2009), bonuses are paid when the top performances are attained, and the performance standards are used to judge whether or not the objectives and the goals were achieved. In contrast, Miles and Miles (2013) argued that there is no distinct connection between the performance of the company and the executive's pay. These studies infer that different companies have different executive bonus and pay policies, where some firms may give their executive bonus and pay based on performance, while others give bonus based on different criteria not including performance. A best practice could be that a sizeable portion of the executive's pay be connected to the overall organization performance and the leadership development of their work teams. Therefore, if the employees are not performing and the company is not productive as they should, a portion of the CEO and executive incentive bonuses and or stock options could be reduced.

B) Stock Options

Stock options support base salary. Giving stock options to employees is good incentive if the options are used appropriately and with ethics. Some companies give employees an option to buy the company stock at a fixed price or at a discount price as an incentive for hiring them. Whenever the employee wishes to use their stock options to purchase the company's shares, as long as it is within the specified timeframe, the company has to release the stock for the employee to purchase. The stock options limits the number of years that shares can be purchased at a specific price. When the employees purchase the company stock, they own a portion of the company. If the value of the company increases, the stock price increases. If an employee sells the stock at the higher price, he or she gains.

A few CEOs have used the stock options unethically and unlawfully by inflating the value of their companies at convenient times so they can gain from the higher value. In this regard they engaged in fraudulent activities to gain an increase in their stock prices. For example, Sanders and Hambrick (2007) noted that "stock options encourage CEOs to place relatively large bets in uncertain investment categories, such as R&D, capital expenditures, and acquisitions" (p. 1056). These investments have no firm surety of a short-term or long-term future return of profit for the company as a whole, and, therefore, the investment risks are higher. Additionally, some investors do not check to see if those investments are generating a return and they later lose their money in unsafe investments. Similarly, Miles and Miles (2013) explained that some executives with large compensations may have an interest in growing and maintaining that sizeable compensation. Therefore, they compromise the development of the organization by engaging in activities that increase their personal earnings instead of increasing the return on investment for the overall organization. To prevent fraud and stimulate performance, the use of corporate governance in organizations is necessary. Corporate governance reduces inappropriate risk taking and inappropriate business activities.

C) Corporate Governance

Organizations have a social responsibility to create efficiency, treat their employees with respect and care, and perform business duties ethically. Employee compensation and pay should be applied with corporate governance, so they are paid what they are worth and according to the weight of the job responsibilities. It is unethical to overload an employee with work and expect the additional work to be done in the same work time and for the same pay. Organizations are governed by civil regulations and compliances applicable to the business field and the markets in which they operate.

Corporate governance is described as ethical measures and mechanisms used to monitoring business transactions whether financial or non-financial. Igor and Chizu (2014) defined governance as a set or organizational systems or habits intended to observe and restrain bad managerial decisions. Similarly, Ahmed and Hamdan (2015) noted that corporate governing is designed to build confidence in the marketplace, develop performance, increase productivity, reduce risks, and attract investors. When employers develop their employees so they are productive, and they feel valued, the employer is exercising corporate governance.

D) Summary

Organizations measure its success through performance, and the company performance is connected to how well the company achieves its goals and objectives. Some executives receive stock options as part of their compensation package. With proper oversight, executives should not be allowed to inflate the price of the stocks or the value of the company to make a personal gain. By facilitating corporate governance in work places employees should be paid the right salary for their work contributions and for the organization to develop the workforce.

CHAPTER 5

A) Develop to Fit

L EADERS SHOULD ASSESS the competency level of each employee, so the employee will be aware of his or her strengths and weaknesses. Competencies and assessment strategies are closely related and are used to complement each other (Chen & Naquin, 2006). When the employee is aware of his or her competency level, they can work to improve the weaker areas and strengthen the stronger areas, especially if their competency is connected to their pay and benefits. Competencies can be strengthened by taking leadership-development and employee-training courses. It is best for employers to fit each employee with their job interest and to provide a route for their career development. Workers should see their job as a means to furthering their professional and personal goals. If they don't, they may leave at the first opportunity.

B) Assessment

Employers should fit each employee with a job appropriate to his or her skills, knowledge, abilities, and perseverance. Assessments are therefore necessary to evaluate the strengths and weaknesses of an employee and to help managers select the right employee for a specific job. Assessments evaluate personality, characteristic, desires, skills, and ability. Assessments can also come in the form of taking math, spelling, and analysis evaluation. The following is a list of ways assessment can be used for job improvement.

1. **Improvement:** Assessment is to be used to assess the level of improvement needed or already attained.
2. **New Employee:** Assessment can be used to fit each new employee with the right organization, the right division, or area of responsibility.
3. **Promotion:** Assessment should also be used to improve employee's skills before or after a promotion.

   a. An employee can be developed to have a number of skills and experiences in a particular area of expertise, so there is a pool of knowledge available for job usage at any time.
   b. Assessment can be done to identify necessary skills needed and then develop those skills that an efficient worker will need in order for him or her to succeed in a new job and for longevity.

4. **Employee Awareness:** Assessment can be done to help an employee know the strength and weaknesses he or she possess, and to understand the job responsibilities and department that he or she will be most valuable in.

There are a variety of assessment tools that are valuable and relevant to evaluate employees, so the employer can link each employee with the right job improvement. Assessments are not the only tools necessary for hiring and improving the organization and the workforce. *360performancesolutions.com* sells assessments and surveys relevant for assessing both the employees and the organization and are also appropriate for benchmarking. Employees can use the individual personality assessment to evaluate their strengths and weaknesses. The personality assessment will also identify the weaker areas that need improvement and the stronger areas that can be strengthened.

C) Benchmarking

An organization can use benchmarking to analyze and measure their products, programs, services, policies, and peer productivity. Benchmarking is a measure that gives a picture of where the organization is and what should be improved. Additionally, benchmarking identifies areas of high performance and low performance. Information from benchmarking can be used to improve weaker areas and to improve overall organizational performance. High-performance areas can be analyzed to identify the best practices. These practices, in turn, can be reengineered and used by other departments performing similar jobs.

High-performing employees and high-performing divisions can be used as a standard to evaluate low-performing employees or low-performing divisions. Benchmarking is not the only tool to be used in improving the organization and improving the workforce – it is one of many tools available. *360performancesolutions.com* consulting provides leadership growth, organization improvement, executive improvement, employee training, and assessment to enable the overall organization to improve and to achieve productive advantages. Included in the assessment programs is a benchmarking tool.

D) Summary

Fitting each hired employee with the job suitable for his or her skills and improvement is a good business strategy. To appropriately select the right employee, assessments should be conducted prior to hiring and during the work life. The knowledge gained from the assessments is to enable the organization to know the strength and weaknesses of the employee so he or she can progress. Benchmarking measures productivity and is an important tool to use to analyze low performing employees versus high-performing ones.

PART 2

I N ORDER FOR organizations to retain good employees, they have to give pay that is sustainable to the employees. Employees are happy workers when they are paid right, and their satisfaction will improve work performance. When the company shows the workers they care about their welfare and increase their pay, their work effort will generate repeat customers and happy customers.

CHAPTER 6

A) How to Negotiate Pay When Moving from One Job to Another

MANY ORGANIZATIONS HAVE different compensation packages to offer potential employees. Some firms offer specific compensation packages for employees with desirable skills and work experiences, regardless of the salary the potential employee earns at their current job. Other employers offer between five to ten percent salary increases to potential new employees who are changing from one job to another.

It is always good for a person to have a record of his or her current pay. Often, an employer will ask a prospective employee his or her current salary as a means to determine if they can afford the hire. Job seekers who are seeking a pay increase should say so. If the person is seeking the same salary, he or she should say so as well. It is necessary for the job seeker to know what he or she wants and the reason for changing their job, so that if an offer is made he or she is not dissatisfied with it. In some instances, a person may decide to accept a job offer with a lower salary because the potential firm offers other attractive benefits.

It is not good to misrepresent your current salary, as human resource departments have a variety of ways to discover this information. If the potential employee is concerned that his or her salary is low, he or she can say that the current industry pays a low rate; and that is one of the reasons why the person is transferring from one job to another.

In my undergraduate years, my organization experienced financial hardships and had to eliminate some departments. My work division was completely eliminated, and I was laid off. I was already a college student taking night courses. I had planned if my job was eliminated, that I would take full-time courses. On the same date I received the separation letter, I went to my university and explained the circumstances and was allowed to take full-time courses. I chose to take the next year to finish my Bachelor's degree. To get my degree finished within that timeframe, I needed to take six classes per semester, which I did, and it was overwhelming. After I graduated, I looked for a full-time job.

During one of my interviews, I was asked what was my last salary. I did not remember, as I did not keep a record of it and had no information on-hand. I put an estimated salary amount on the application form, and later was offered the job. The salary they offered me was an increase of five percent over my last estimated salary. I accepted their offer. About two years later, I was tossing out unwanted documents and papers when I stumbled across my pay stubs from the job I had before full-time studies. When I reviewed the pay stubs, my last salary was about three thousand dollars more than what I had quoted. I was making a lower salary than I had at my last job. There was nothing I could do to change my current salary – I couldn't go back after having provided inaccurate information. I learned from that experience, and never made that mistake again. I became very savvy in negotiating my salary and asking for what I was worth. Fortunately, I sought out promotions within my organization and was able to move up, receiving salary increases with each new position.

I continued my education by going to school part-time at nights, eventually completing my Master's degree. One of these promotions increased my salary to a little over $10,000, because the lowest salary for that new job was a little over $10,000 of my current job title. That was the rate for the position, and could not be any less. Therefore, it is relevant to know that some employers do look at the last salary to decide how much to offer a potential employee. Workers should be aware of this, so they can help the potential employer decide on a suitable compensation package for them.

B) Summary

When negotiating salary, it is good to say that you are looking for a higher salary increase than you currently have so the employer will know what offer to make to you. It is also good to know how much you are making or have made in past employment so you will provide accurate information when asked.

CHAPTER 7

A) How to Ask for a Pay Raise

EMPLOYEES SHOULD HAVE the courage and confidence to ask for a pay raise as they take on more and more responsibilities. Kennett (2012) explained that pay increases should be requested, even though it is an intimidating prospect, because the employee was given an added workload from a vacant position, or a new initiative. The additional workload taken on saves the employer money, as there is a reduction of expense for the employer and an increased workload for the employee. Consequently, getting a small percentage of that savings from the vacant position is not an unjust request, as the work is being done and the employee is fulfilling dual positions.

If an employee was given additional work from a new initiative, or has been performing well with no financial incentive, it is beneficial to make a salary increase request although he or she does not know what the outcome will be. Some employers illegally pay male workers more than female employees for the same job responsibilities (Kenneth, 2012). If this is the case, it is justifiable to request a salary increase. Sometimes, it is not that the employer is unwilling to increase pay: it could be that the boss is waiting for the employee to ask. Often, employees are timid or feel too self-conscious to make this request.

B) Document Your Work Accomplishments

To improve one's chances of getting the pay raise, it is good to record the work responsibilities, work ethics, and work accomplishments, then present it in the negotiation. OfficePro (2008) stated that, on occasion, a supervisor or a boss may be unaware of all the different layers of the employee job responsibilities. It is beneficial to give the boss a weekly report that identifies the projects being worked on, and the completed work initiatives. When the manager or supervisor sees this documentation, he or she will know that the employee is efficient, valuable, productive, a leader, and is contributing to the overall success of the organization.

Work engagement is what leaders want from employees. Engagement supports an organization to thrive. Before asking for a raise, an employee is to present all completed work assignments. This presentation should be clearly organized and presented in chronological order (OfficePro, 2008). Having specific information about the work contributions will demonstrate that the employee is serious and has facts connected to the salary-increase request. The boss may use these facts to determine if the employee is worthy of the raise, or how the company can enable the employee to develop more so he or she can justify a pay raise.

When the employee is asking for a pay raise, the boss will review the employee's work performance standards and work etiquette. This means that the manager will evaluate if the employee is respectful of others' time, effort, and personality. In addition, the supervisor will ensure that the employee does not demoralize, disturb, embarrass, or aggravate others (Anderson, 2015). In assessing the employee's contribution, the boss will also review complaints and compliments. The boss may also evaluate how the worker makes efforts to correct mistakes, develops ad grow through work situations, and interacts with other workers. In light of all that the boss may evaluate, it is best to prepare oneself in advance before asking for a pay raise.

Look for emails that the boss has complemented you for a good job done, or from co-workers or customers who appreciated and said the information helped them understand clearly a process or procedure, etc. Use these email as proof that the job is processed appropriately and providing value to the organization. Additionally, if your immediate past performance appraisals are good, use it as well to justify your work ethics and work productivity.

C) When is the Best Time to Ask for a Pay Raise?

Based on the workload and other changes that affect the employee, he or she can prepare to ask for a pay raise within a few weeks or a month, depending on the urgency of the situation that the worker has to handle. However, it is best to think about asking for a pay raise at least six months before the worker actually makes the request. Preparing in advance, enables the worker to correct any known issues, prepare concrete documentation, and ensure the boss satisfaction with the employee's recent performance. An employee should build credibility in his or her work efforts and integrity in his or her personality so that there is a valid reason to request the pay raise. Additionally, while making the necessary improvements, the worker is developing and connecting to the organization and the work environment.

D) Identify Your Weaknesses

In looking at these guidelines, the employee should identify where he or she does not have adequate documentation and credibility. The employee should work on improving weak areas, so that, when the request is made, the boss and other colleagues will know that the worker is an engaging team player who is developing himself or herself to match the organization. The employee could also ask the boss to offer suggestions for improvement, so the worker can develop greater proficiency. By speaking with the boss and requesting feedback, the employee both demonstrates and documents her or his interest in improving. The conversation with the boss will also demonstrate that the employee is trying to have a stronger connection to the division, mission, and goals of the work area. Developing oneself before asking for a pay raise gives the worker credibility and a proven track record, allowing them to demonstrate their contributions and growth.

E) Seek Out Appropriate Training and Development Programs

Employees seeking to develop skills and knowledge can use the internal training programs, or seek outside education geared toward the competencies they hope to possess. The employer may pay for an outside development program, or the employee could pay from his or her private funds. Despite adequate preparation, the raise may not be approved. Therefore, the employee should be prepared to negotiate other compensation factors until the company can provide a pay raise.

When employees are growing in an organization and are connected to its goals, their work output and interactions with others will demonstrate this growth. Anderson (2015) said that the employees who are developing exhibit this through their work effort, their fufillment of responsibilities, and their feedback from leaders, colleagues, and customers. They should also demonstrate teamwork and team player participation and show that their career development path is progressing.

Employees should manage their careers by taking training courses offered by the employer, requesting new assignments to enable their knowledge to develop, or asking for a mentor who they can shadow while developing a skill set and learning how to handle more advanced work responsibilities. Employees have their future in their hands. They should put forth the effort to grow, develop, and incorporate changes in their professional life to enable promotion and more innovative work assignments. Inventive work assignments help the mind to develop, allowing the employee to think outside of the box, and approach problem-solving from different perspectives.

Sometimes, work overload can cause the career development of an individual to be stifled. If this is the case, the employee should have documentation of the issues, identify all work responsibilities and the timeline to get the work completed, and ask the boss for help from other employees who may not be as busy. If this is not possible, it may be necessary for the manager to hire a new person to take on some of the overbearing responsibilities.

F) Be Prepared: Write out the Script of What to Say

In preparing to ask for a pay raise, the employee should write out a script of what to say. Kenneth (2012) emphasized that "Your tone of voice is also important in making a successful bid for a higher salary. Practice what you're going to say. You need to sound confident and competent, not aggressive or aggrieved (p. 66)." When making a presentation, your personal demeanor is connected to your speech. It is, therefore, worthwhile to put more effort into preparing for the discussion instead of expecting to just wing it.

These are a few of the scripts that could be used in the salary increase discussion. Send an email to the boss or supervisor and say: "I would like to meet with you regarding a personal situation; please let me know when you will be available to discuss this", or "I would like to meet with you to discuss my compensation." At the discussion table say, "I enjoy my job, and I can identify my accomplishments for the past 6-months or past year. My work contribution has been valuable to the success of this department in achieving its objectives, and in support of the goal of this organization. Based on my performance, or work load, I believe a salary increase of 15% is reasonable." It is good to ask for a higher increase so there is room for your boss to negotiate what he or she can afford. Expect the boss to object to the salary increase, so remain confident and show enthusiasm in your tone and demeanor no matter what the response is.

G) Summary

Employees should have the confidence to request pay increases when they have contributed to the success of the department, and also when they have additional assignments that are of higher responsibility. It is good to prepare one mentally and physically to ask for a pay increase and to have all the right documents ready. It is recommended that preparing and documenting your work achievements should take between 6 months to one year. Ask for training and development you would like to take that is connected to your job and your career goals. Write out a script of what to say to ask for a pay increase and practice it.

CHAPTER 8

A) When is the Best Time to Approach Your Boss for a Pay Raise?

IT IS GOOD for the employee to calculate the best time to discuss a pay raise with his or her boss. It is best to set up the meeting when the boss is not busy or is relaxed. The boss may be more relaxed in the morning than the afternoon, or vice versa. Therefore, an employee should know the boss and what works best for him or her, in order to successfully discuss the pay increase. Additionally, OfficePro (2008) noted that a good time to request a pay increase is right after the employee has successfully finished a work project. In this case, the boss would be pleased with the worker's time and effort and may be more open to discussion. Asking for a pay raise needs proper planning, proper execution, and the proper timing.

B) What if the Boss Says That There is No Budget for a Pay Raise?

Many possibilities can occur when meeting with the boss. Employees should not plan to use the threat of leaving their employment if they do not get the desired salary increase (Bullmore, 2012). If the situation is bad enough to warrant leaving, the worker should look for another place of employment without using threats. If the employee decides to leave, he or she should leave in a cordial manner and on good terms. The employee should try to prepare in advance of the salary increase negotiation for other options that may be of benefit and doable, to which the boss may more readily agree.

Many organizations go through a period of financial difficulties. If a company is going through hardship at a time when the employee is overburdened with work, the worker should be prepared to hear the boss say that the company does not have a salary increase in the budget at this time (Zeimer, 2015). In some situations, the boss may not want to grant a salary increase. The employee should have already thought about the different possible scenarios that could be introduced during this negotiation, and be prepared to hear the views of the boss, whether they are good or bad.

If the boss says that the company cannot afford a salary increase at this time, or if the answer is just plain "no," the employee should have a list of other benefits that he or she can negotiate while waiting for the finances to improve or for the time to make another request. An employee can negotiate with the boss to get a meaningful bonus at the end of the year, to gain knowledge, to have a valuable mentor, and to learn some of the parts of another employee's job that he or she may be interested in. The employee can ask to be able to work on Saturdays, or to have a more flexible work schedule where he or she can arrive at a convenient time for him or her and leave at a later time – maybe 11:00 a.m. to 6 p.m. instead of 9:00 a.m. to 4:00 p.m. and other variations of that flexibility. Kenneth (2012) explained that employees can also negotiate "having extra paid holiday [vacation] or working at home some days of the week" (p.66). Employees can also ask for improvement bonus and stock options depending on the organization. Consequently, the idea is to come up with solutions that are realistic and possible, so that the boss can have a few items to think about in supporting a part of the worker's interest.

The boss may be willing to consider a salary increase, but might first want to see that the employee can handle responsibilities demanding greater critical-thinking and problem-solving skills. Bosses may also ask that the employee take on additional work assignments and complete them successfully, or that the worker shoulder more difficult responsibilities, before the management team considers increasing the salary (Zeimer, 2015). Such a response could indicate that there is money for a salary increase, but the boss may need to justify it to higher leaders. The boss may also want to prevent jealousy among colleagues by showing that the worker has taken on additional assignments to justify his or her pay increase.

Another possible scenario could come of this negotiation: the boss could say that the employee is not as developed in his or her career, or underdeveloped in handling multiple responsibilities, and that the employee should improve his or her skills. In this case, the worker should prepare beforehand to see what training courses are available, or ask the boss to suggest the best courses to take. Zeimer (2015) indicated that the boss might offer a management certification training to the employee. The employer may suggest that, upon completion, promotion will be considered.

A properly-prepared employee will know what training programs are of interest to his or her long-term career development, and be capable of discussing this with the boss. The boss may also say that the employee can only take courses that are connected to the company's long-term goals. Gaining development that matches the organization is not a bad incentive. It is a negotiation tool for future promotion while the employee is learning and developing to be a leader wherever he or she may go in the future.

C) How to Deal with No Pay Raise

Although the worker put a lot of time and effort into preparing for the salary negotiation and did not get one, the employee has gained from the preparation, has learned how to negotiate, and is developing confidence. There may be a salary increase for the employee not so far down the road. If the answer is a "no," or there is no money in the budget, then the employee should articulate to the boss that as soon as the hindrance has cleared, the employee will be expecting the salary increase (Kenneth, 2012). The employee could also ask the boss when he or she may make another request for a salary raise. This discussion helps the boss to expect another salay increase request from the employee. Therefore, the boss will proactively prepare to request more funding in the upcoming budget negotiation.

D) Summary

Ask for a pay raise when things are running smoothly, at a convenient time for the boss, and when you have successfully completed a project. If the boss says there can't be any pay increase, then the employee can negotiate for bonus, flexible work hours and other necessary perks that are satisfactory until they can get an increase. The employee can also choose to get development whether on the job or off the job in the meanwhile. The employee should also articulate to the boss that as soon as the organization is back to normal that he or she expects the pay increase.

CHAPTER 9

A) What to Do After Speaking with Your Boss for a Pay Raise

EMPLOYEES SHOULD SEND a follow-up email, identifying improvements they plan to engage in while anticipating a promotion or a salary increase. The email is not designed to get a "yes" from the employer, but to document the negotiation, and the worker's desire to improve. The worker should follow up with any proposed improvements, and document his or her progress. Additionally, after the employee has completed training, the lessons learned should be incorporated into his or her professional and personal life. In this way, the employee can have a well-rounded development and be truly efficient at everything he or she engages in.

B) Salary Guides

In order to know what an employee is worth, it is best to look at a salary guide for that year. Salary increases from year to year, but in some cases can drop due to economic constraints and recession. A good website for salary comparison is *http://salary.com/*. On this site, you can browse popular salaries by industry, category, and much more. Additionally, an employee can also look at the annual Palmer Group salary guide at *http://www.thepalmergroup.com/support/PDFs/SalaryGuide.pdf.* This site provides low and high range salary comparison chart for many different positions. Other sites are *http://glassdoor.com* and *http://payscale.com*.

WORDS OF UPLIFTMENT

- We develop employees so that we are fully developed.

- We give so that others may have.

- Giving allows others to have and to be developed.

- Development is the key to growth.

- When we do not develop, we are truncated.

- Truncation causes immaturity, which results in poor performance.

- We must be selfless when we develop for the good of all.

- Productivity is doing the work that fulfills the requirement.

- Productivity leads to good performance and productive advantage.

- Productive advantage generates more profit.

- Employee productivity reflects the development of the leadership.

- Unproductivity is a reflection of poor leadership.

- Undermining and harsh criticisms reduce productivity.

- Motivation is energy activated, which leads to a reward.

- Motivation influences development.

- Shadowing is learning and exchanging techniques about other job skills.

- Mentoring is developing a work relationship with an apprentice, in order to transfer knowledge with integrity.

- Mentoring and shadowing increase motivation.

- Provide work tools and opportunities for creativity that are specific to work environments.

- Empower workers to use creativity.

CONCLUSION

I N CONCLUSION, ORGANIZATIONS demonstrate that they value their employees at all levels by acknowledging their work efforts and their contributions to the organization's improvement and success. Some firms recognize the work of their employees through various compensation methods, including rewards, benefits, and incentives.

Compensation can take different forms for different companies, including performance-, skill-, and team-based pay. While research has shown performance-based pay to be effective in generating a higher work output, others have noted that employees may engage in unethical behaviors in an attempt to garner rewards. Skill-based pay, in which greater skill yields more compensation, has, according to Murray and Gerhart (1998), motivated workers to increase their skill level. Team-based pay has been demonstrated to increase cooperation, integration, problem-solving, and development. Moreover, employees rewarded as a team do not compete with each other. Additionally, cash bonuses and other incentives can be offered to reward good work and encourage continuing success. Besides monetary payment, these incentives can take the form of paid vacation time, stock options, and gain sharing.

Executives and administrators, like all other employees, should be appropriately compensated to ensure the health of their organization. In order to monitor executives, a board of directors can be selected by shareholders. The board of directors ensures that the firm's financials are in order, and manages the CEO. A company's executives can earn compensation in the form of base salary along with fringe benefits, stock options, and bonuses, while the board approves the executives' compensations.

The government has instituted compliance methodologies to prevent fraud and mismanagement. These measures will ensure that companies report accurate financial standings so the public can make informed decisions. Firms should assess their employees to know their strengths and weaknesses. Such evaluation helps employees grow, meet their goals, and better enjoy their work environment.

Workers must recognize the vital role they play in the success of their company. An organization cannot develop or grow without the work efforts of its employees. The employees help the organization grow and develop to be profitable and sustainable. The employees can transfer their services to other organizations at their desire, and an organization cannot do that, as it is not transferable. Therefore, the relationship between the organization and its employees should be collaborative, supportive, and respectful. Finding and retaining talented and motivated people is essential to the performance of any company. Motivating employees to perform their jobs to the best of their ability may determine an organization's success or failure.

Compensation and recognition are, therefore, critical elements in a company's strategy for hiring and keeping essential personnel. It is the human resources responsibility to understand compensation strategy, and to be familiar with the full array of compensation plans, and associated benefits, available to employees within the scope of operation.

It is also valuable to appreciate the ways compensation programs may influence desired performance.

Workers should know how to ask for a salary increase and how to prepare for this negotiation. This negotiation must be timed properly, and employees should ideally prepare several months in advance. Employees should ideally follow up with any performance or improvement plans suggested for growth before asking for a raise. Such improvement helps employees grow, meet their goals, and better enjoy their work environment. Furthermore, continuing education or training is necessary, so the employee's value and contribution is increased.

It is helpful for an employee to bring documents identifying the contributions he or she makes to the company, and to present this in negotiation. The salary increase negotiation can be an intimidating one. However, when workers become aware of their worth to an organization, they will understand when a raise is justified. When employees are properly compensated, both companies and workers stand to benefit.

GLOSSARY

Assessments - evaluate personality, characteristic, desires, skills, and ability Audit committee monitors the honesty of the financial statements and the internal audit roles

Benchmarking - measure that gives a picture of where the organization is and what should be improved

Board of Directors - monitor the executive leaders, approve major investments, hire the executive team, approve acquisitions, create executives' compensations, oversee financial reports, and protect the concerns of the shareholders

Business strategy - long-term goal with steps of how to meet customer needs, how to generate revenues, and to sustain productive advantages in the market

Cash incentive payments - encouragement for continued job success and accomplishments

Chief Executive Officer (CEO) - ensures that the firm is running smoothly, meet strategic objectives and goals, budgets are managed, fiscal plans are appropriate, and productive advantages are achieved

Compensation - comprised of many different types of rewards systems include base pay, incentive, merit, vacation, sick pay, health insurance, and such things as cell phone or car allowance

Compensation committee - handles the executive compensation

Competency - having motives, beliefs, traits, skills, and attitudes that are connected to work-related activities

Corporate governance - ethical measures and mechanisms used to monitoring business transactions whether financial or non-financial

Engagement - worker is occupied with accomplishing the work tasks, is enthusiastic about work

Internal audit - a committee that counsels the general counsel, human resource, risk officer, board members, and CEO ensure compliance

Internal auditor - prevents earnings management by the executives

Line person - performs the core work responsibilities of the firm such as sales or production.

Mission statement - says the purpose of the organization, the goals the organization will accomplish, and the steps to take to get them completed

Optimal performance and function - the employee puts forth full effort, critical thinking, critical analysis, and his or her best to accomplish the objectives of the organization

Staff person - plays a supporting role such as human resource officer, or office manager.

Stock Options - firms giving their employees an option to buy the company stock at a fixed price or at a discount price as an incentive for hiring them

Team collectivism - where the team supports one another and work together to fulfill the objectives of the organization

Total rewards - a mixture of compensation, rewards, and work experience

Vision statement - says where the company is heading for the present and future and the core values such as, what the firm believes in, its expectations, and the culture of the firm

REFERENCES

Anderson, E. (2015). Four ways to tell if your employees are keepers. *Forbes.* p.1. Retrieved from *http://www.forbes.com*

Appelbaum, S. H., & Mackenzie, L. (1996). Compensation in the year 2000: Pay for performance? *Health Manpower Management. 23*(3), 31-39. doi:1108/09552069610125919

Berk, J., & DeMarzo, P. (2014). *Corporate Finance.* (3rd Ed.). Boston, MA. Pearson Education, Inc.

Bostan, I., & Grosu, V. (2010). The Role of internal audit in optimization of corporate governance at the groups of companies. *Theoretical & Applied Economics. 17*(2). 89-110. Retrieved from http://www. ectap.ro

Bullmore, J. (2012). What's your problem. *Management Today. 65.* Retrieved from http://www.mgmt2day.griet.ac.in/

Chen, H.C., & Naquin, S. S. (2006). An integrative model of competency development, training design, assessment center, and multi-rater assessment. *Advances in Developing Human Resources, 8*(2), 265-282. doi:1177/1523422305286156

Gagné, M., & Forest, J. (2008). The study of compensation systems through the lens of self-determination theory: Reconciling 35 years of debate. *Canadian Psychology, 49*(3), 225-232. 232. *doi*:1037/a0012757

Gross, S., Bundy, K., Johnson, R. (2011). The ongoing integration of total rewards. *Employee Relations Today. 37*(4), 11 17. doi:10.1002/ ert.20316

Haines III, V. Y., & Tagger, S. (2006). Antecedents of team reward attitude. *Group Dynamics: Theory, Reward, and Practice, 10*(3), 194-205. doi 1108/02683940910952705

Hameed, A., Ramzan, M., Ali, G., Arslan, M. (2014). Impact of Compensation on Employee Performance: Empirical Evidence from Banking Sector of Pakistan. *International Journal of Business and Social Science* 5(2). 302-309. Retrieved from http://ijbssnet.com/journals

Harvey, M. (1993). Designing a global compensation system: The logic and a model. *Columbia Journal of World Business, 28*(4), 56-72. doi:1016/0022-5428(93)90006-B

Hoffman, H. (2014). Salaries vs. benefits: What employee compensation can tell us. *Statesman Journal.* Retrieved from *http://www. statesmanjournal.com/story/news/politics/state-workers /9845193*

International Financial Law Review. (2009). The US Sarbanes-Oxley Act of 2002. *Securities,* 45-58. Retrieved from *http://www.iflr.com/ Corporate-archive.html*

Ionescu, I.; Damoc, C., & Rusu, R. (2015). Corporate governance in Romania: Necessity or bureaucracy? *Audit Financiar. 13*(127), 126-135. Retrieved from *http://revista.cafr.ro*

Kennett, M. (2012). First class coach._*Management Today.* 66-66. Retrieved from *http://www.mgmt2day.griet.ac.in/*

Kiyani, A., Akhtar, S., & Haroon, M. *(2011)* Impact of monetary rewards on achievement of employee's personal goals. *RMIC, 4*(10), 58-69. *Retrieved from http://www.intellectbase.org/RMIC.php*

Laux, C., & Laux, V. (2009). Board committees, CEO compensation, and earnings management. *The Accounting Review. 84(3)*, 869-891. doi:2308/accr.2009.84.3.869

Lawler III, E. E. (1995). The new pay: A strategic approach. *Compensation & Benefits Review, 27*(4), 14-22. doi:1177/088636879502700608

Levy, S.; Mitchell, H.; Guled, C., & Guled, J. (2010). Total reward: Pay and pension contributions in the private and public sectors. *Economic & Labor Market Review 4*(9), 22-28. doi:1057/elmr.2010.126

Miles, P. C., & Miles, G. (2013). Corporate social responsibility and executive compensation: Exploring the link. *Social Responsibility Journal 9*(1), 76-90. Retrieved from *https://faculty.unt.edu/editprofile.php*

Murray, B., & Gerhart, B. (1998). An empirical analysis of a skill-based pay program and plant performance outcomes. *Academy of Management Journal, 41*(1), 68-78. doi:2307/256898

OfficePro (2008). Asking for a raise. *Robert Half 68*(5), 9. Retrieved from *https://www.roberthalf.com/finance/blog/asking-for-a-raise-like-a-pro*

Pollane, R. A. (2014). Performance measurement and control systems evidence from Canada. *International Journal of Business, Accounting, & Finance 8*(1), 79-97. Retrieved from *http://www.theijbm.com*

Ramamoorti, S., & Balakrishnan, U.R. (2010). Carrots and Sticks. *Internal Auditor. 67*(5), 61-65. Retrieved from *https://na.theiia.org/periodicals/Pages/Periodicals*

Sanders, G.W.M., & Hambrick, D. C., (2007). Swinging for the fences: The effects of CEO stock options on company risks-taking and performance. *Academy of Management Journal, 50*(5), 1055–1078. 50(5), 1055-1078. *doi*:5465/AMJ.2007.27156438

Sheng-Syan; C. & Chia-Wei, H. (2013) The Sarbanes-Oxley Act, earnings management, and post-buyback performance of open-market repurchasing firms. *Journal of Financial & Quantitative Analysis. 48*(6), 1847-1876. 30p. doi:1017/S0022109014000040.

Wood, R. E., (2004). How independent is your compensation committee? *Benefits Law Journal. 17*(4), 82-97. Retrieved from *http://lawlib.wlu.edu/LJ/.*

Zeimer, G. (2015). What to say when you must decline a pay raise request. *Communication Briefings. 34*(8), 5-5. Retrieved from *http://blog.intuit.com.*

INDEX